Playing Your Tiny Harp

I0801782

Laurie Riley
&
Lorna Govier

Roosebeck Walnut Baby Harp 12-String (HPBYW) cover image courtesy of Ensoul Music Designs, Inc.

MEL BAY

WWW.MELBAY.COM

Contents

About the Authors

Laurie Riley is a popular harp performer and teacher whose many instructional books and DVDs have been used by students worldwide since 1990. Her many CDs and YouTube videos feature traditional, ethnic, and contemporary music, as well as her own compositions on the Celtic harp, the rare double-strung harp, and the historical wire-strung harp. Laurie's website is www.laurieriley.com

Lorna Govier is a longtime harpist, harp music lover, and music scholar. She has transcribed the music for Laurie Riley's books *Composed in Heart* and *Advanced Compositions for the Double Strung Harp*. She has recorded two albums: one Celtic, *The Bright Green Bough*, and one for ancient middle eastern lyre with Dr. Anne Kilmer, *The Silver Lyre*. Her website is www.southwestharp.com

Introduction

A "tiny harp" may have 8, 12, 15, 18 or 22 strings. Although very small compared to most other harps, you can play beautiful music on a tiny harp.

This book is for those who have never played a harp before. You may wish to play by ear, or perhaps you want to read music. You may prefer to improvise, to play tunes you know, or to learn new tunes. All of that is possible on your tiny harp, as long as you keep it properly tuned.

Accessories You Should Have

• Tuning Key: A small wrench comes with the harp and is used for turning the tuning pegs to tune your strings by tightening or loosening the strings to the appropriate pitches.

• Electronic harp tuner: available at any music store. (See the section "Tuning Your Harp".)

• Protective cover: if the harp did not come with one, you can make one from a suitcase or a quilted sleeping bag. Use it whenever you travel with your harp.

Caring for Your Harp

• The strings of a harp stretch and will go out of tune over time with temperature and humidity changes, or simply from playing them; you will likely have to tune your harp at least twice a day when it is new. After a new harp "settles" (in a few weeks), tune it at least once a week.

• Always keep your harp tuned to "concert" pitch (the pitch setting on an electronic tuner should be A = 440).

• Your harp should be kept away from direct sunlight and other sources of heat.

• Never leave your harp in a hot car.

• Never let your harp get wet, and never store it in a humid place.

• When traveling, always put your harp in a protective case.

• To polish the wood of the harp, use guitar polish, not furniture polish, and don't get it on the strings.

• Strings do not need to be changed unless they break. If they break often, please see the section on "String Breakage" and take appropriate action.

• Get your levers regulated if they are not accurate (see the section on levers)

• To protect the warranty, always have maintenance and repairs done by the company that made the harp, unless they are located overseas; in which case repairs should be done by a qualified luthier.

• Most harps come with extra strings. If yours did not, order a spare set from Robinson's Harp Shop in Mt. Laguna, California or from Vermont Strings. They make strings for all sizes of harps.

String Breakage

Nylon strings sometimes break. If it happens once in a while, that's normal. If it happens often, that is **not** normal. Possible reasons for excessive string breakage are:

- The harp has been left in a hot place or in direct sunlight. Always keep it in the shade and away from heaters.
- The strings have been improperly tuned - be sure to read the tuning instructions that came with your harp.
- The hardware that comes in contact with the strings may have rough spots. If the same strings break again and again after being replaced, use 500-grit sandpaper to smoothe all the hardware that those strings pass over or through.
- The harp came with improperly gauged strings. Contact Robinson's Harp Shop in Mt. Laguna CA, or from Vermont Srings and get a properly gauged set.

How to change a string:

1. Remove the broken string and save it for reference (see step 3).
2. Find the appropriate new string (refer to the string chart that came with your harp, or get the appropriate chart from Robinson's Harp Shop, or Vermont Strings).
3. Tie a firm knot in one end of the new string, using the same kind of knot that you see on the string that broke. The knot should be large enough so it will not pull through the string hole on the harp, or it should have a bead or small leather disc attached to keep it from pulling through.
4. Grab the other end of the string and, from the inside of the back of the harp, put the end through the string hole, and then pull it through from the front.
5. Thread the string through the hole in the pin at the top and pull it taut.
6. Using your tuning key, start turning the pin so the string winds onto the pin in the same direction the other strings are wound. As you turn, be sure the string-end goes under the first winding of the string to hold it in place; otherwise it will just pull through the hole and the string will not tighten.
7. When the string is taut, tune it to the proper pitch (see next section).
8. The new string will go out of tune right away and you will have to keep tuning it every little while until it starts to hold its pitch.

Tuning Your Harp

To tune the harp, you should use an electronic tuner, available at any music store. The tuner will ensure that you tune accurately. To use your electronic tuner, go to a quiet room and turn the power button on. If there is any extraneous noise in the room, it will affect the tuner, so do not talk while tuning.

The harp should be tuned to "concert pitch", which is "A = 440" on the electronic tuner setting.

There are a few options for how to tune your harp:

Tuning to a scale that sounds pretty:

If you have never played before and you want to make music right away, a lovely scale called "pentatonic" has all the notes automatically in harmony with each other. The notes of this scale are:

C(red) D F F(blue) G A C C(red).

Tuning to a normal "do-re-mi" scale:

A do-re-mi or diatonic scale consists of the notes C D E F G A B. The notes of a C major scale start on a red string and go up from there. This scale repeats as you continue up the strings:

C(red) D E F(blue) G A B, C(red) D E F(blue) G A B, C(red) D E F(blue) G A B

The strings of your harp should be color-coded with the C notes red and the F notes blue, thusly: C(red) D E F(blue) G A B. Some tiny harps come with random colors, in which case contact Robinson's Harp Shop, Vermont Strings, or another reputable string maker to get a proper string set.

When a string is not in tune, its pitch is either too low or too high. If you cannot tell by listening, the electronic tuner indicates whether it is low or high, and by how much. When it is too low, it is "flat", and when it is too high, it is "sharp".

To tune a string, pluck it and compare it to the tuner. If it is not at the proper pitch, pluck it again and turn the tuning peg while it is ringing. Keep plucking and tuning until it is in tune. Never turn a tuning peg when the string is not ringing – you won't know how far to turn the peg if you can't hear the pitch changing, and you may break strings that way.

How To Hold Your Tiny Harp

The parts of your harp are:

- soundbox - the hollow, box-like part
- pillar - the support section that does not have strings attached
- neck – the curved section at the top with tuning pegs where the strings are attached
- shoulder – where the neck and body meet

Hold the harp with the neck at the top and the soundbox close to your right shoulder. The shortest strings will be closest to you.

Plucking the Strings

On most harps, the melody is usually played with the right hand, and accompaniment with the left hand. On a tiny harp, you can hold the harp with one hand and play it with the other if you wish.

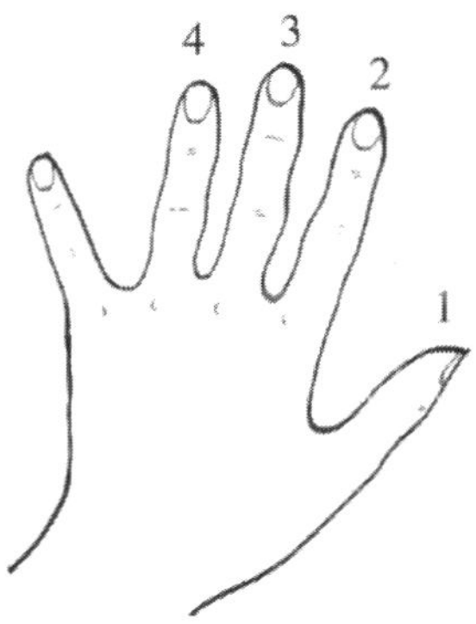

Your fingers are numbered this way:

1 = thumb
2 = forefinger
3 = middle finger
4 = ring finger

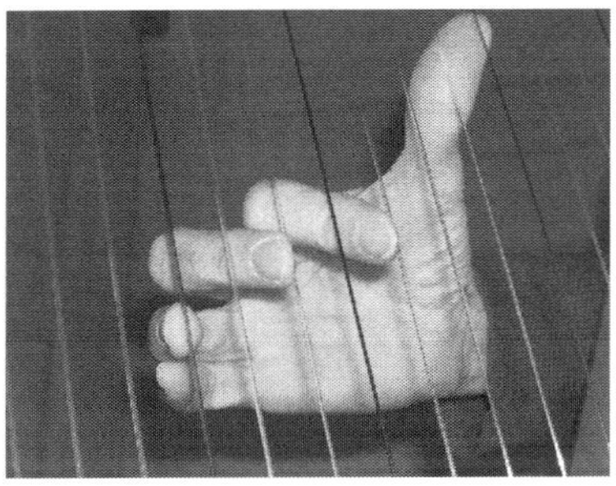

Let's start with the right hand. Place the thumb and three fingertips on the strings, as in the photo. With the third finger, pull the string toward you slightly and release it, closing the finger directly into the palm of your hand. Keep the other fingers on the strings!

Next, *keeping the third finger in the palm of your hand*, pluck with the second finger and close it into the palm. Be sure to keep the thumb placed on its string.

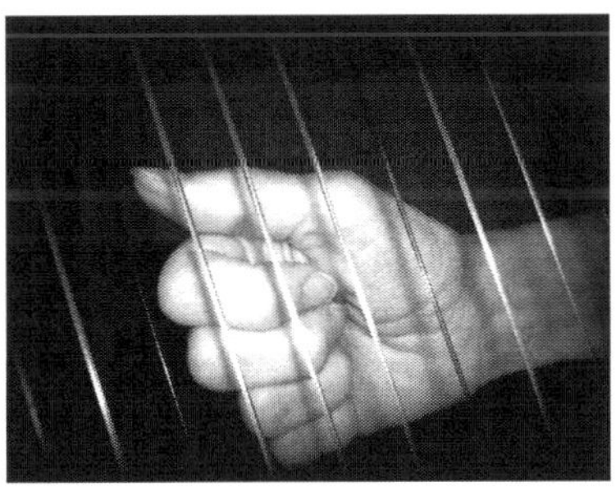

Now the thumb should pluck and close over the the index finger. You'll end up with your hand in a *relaxed* fist, as in this photo.

This is how your hand should look whenever you finish plucking a phrase or chord (see terminology on the following page).

You can also practice these plucking movements using four fingers rather than just three.

Terminology

What are chords? A chord consists of three or more notes sounding together.

What is a scale? A scale is a set of notes, represented by the strings of your harp. Your harp is tuned to a C scale; in other words, the scale starts on the C note (red string) and progresses thusly: C, D, E, F, G, A, B, and C.

What is an interval? When two notes are played at the same time, the term "interval" refers to the distance between them. For instance, choose a note (string) and call it "one", and then choose
another note (string) and count how many strings there are between the two, *plus both of the strings you've chosen*. The number you count is the interval. If, for instance, there are five strings, the interval is a *fifth.* If there are three strings, it's a *third*, and so on. (Look at the second illustration in the section "Plucking the Strings"; the index finger (finger 32) and thumb (finger #1) are placed on an interval of a third.)

What is an exercise? An exercise is used for the purpose of getting the fingers and brain accustomed to playing certain sequences, patterns, and techniques. Practicing exercises is absolutely essential to becoming a good harp player.

What is a phrase? A phrase is a group of notes that complete a musical thought, much like the words between commas in a written sentence. Phrases are not defined by measures.

What is a repertoire? A repertoire is a collection of tunes that you know and can play well. Every harp player works to develop a repertoire.

How to Read Standard Music Notation

Music notation is a system of symbols that tell you what notes to play and how long the notes are relative to each other. It's important to know the basics of reading notation in order to correctly read and play the tunes in this book, so be sure to study this section carefully!

The Staff: The staff is the set of horizontal lines on which the notes and symbols appear. In harp music there are two sets of five lines each, called *staves* ("staves" is the plural of "staff"). The lines AND the spaces between them represent strings on the harp. In other words, each line *and* each space is a string, and the larger space between the upper and lower set of lines represents three strings. (See the illustration.)

Measures: A measure is the space between each vertical line on the staff. It helps you to count the beat of the notes contained within it.

Clefs: Usually, two clefs are used to notate harp music:

Treble Clef

Bass Clef

Harp music notation usually shows two clefs on a staff. The treble clef is for the right hand, and the bass clef is for the left hand.

The reason the two clefs are called by different names is because they are read differently. The scale of notes can be visualized on the staff as starting on the lowest string of your harp (represented by the lowest note appearing in the bass clef), ascending through the bass clef and continuing through the treble clef. (Some harps have more strings than this; some have fewer.)

In this illustration, the line representing middle C does not show on actual notation, but you can imagine that it does.

However, for ease of reading and because this book is for tiny harps with a limited range, two treble staves will be used for notation of music for two hands; the upper stave represents notes to be played by the right hand, and the lower stave represents notes for the left.

Time Signatures: *Time signatures look like fractions, but they are not! It is impossible to play music correctly from notation without understanding what the time signature symbol means and how to use it.*

Contrary to what is often assumed, the time signature does *not* tell you how fast the music should be played (tempo). It only tells you the value of the notes and how many beats there are in each measure. *The top number indicates the number of beats per measure, and the bottom number indicates what kind of note gets one beat.*

For the bottom number, when you see 4 it means *quarter note*, or when you see 8 it means *eighth note.*

For instance, in the time signature 4/4, there are 4 beats per measure (top number) and a *quarter note* equals one beat (the number 4 means quarter note). 4/4 time may also be indicated with a symbol that looks like a C, meaning "common time".

In the time signature 3/4, there are 3 beats per measure and a quarter note gets one beat.

In the time signature 6/8, there are 6 beats per measure and an eighth note gets one beat.

Counting the beat is essential in playing music correctly. A whole note = 2 half notes = 4 quarter notes = 8 eighth notes = 16 sixteenth notes.

Be sure to give each note you play the value indicated by paying attention to the time signature.

Do not pause between measures. Count evenly.

When there is a time signature of ¾ each measure would be counted "**one**, two, three" (beat **one** is louder). Each measure of a piece with a time signature of 4/4 would be counted "**one**, two, three, four". In 3/4 time each measure would be counted "**one**, two, three". For a piece in 6/8 time, count "one, two, three, **four,** five, six".

Use a metronome (available in any music store or as a cell phone app) when learning to count time signatures. A metronome makes an audible click that can be set to whatever tempo (speed) you wish to play. Some metronomes beep; which is harder to hear when you are playing than an unpitched woodblock sound or click. Be sure to get a metronome that clicks rather than beeps.

The Notes:

In music notation you will see different kinds of notes. The difference in how they look indicates their "value" relative to each other; in other words, how many beats they each get. If all notes had the same value, all music would be very stilted and uninteresting.

Here are the types of notes:

WHOLE NOTE

HALF NOTE (has a time value of one half of a whole note)

QUARTER NOTE (has a time value of one fourth of a whole note)

EIGHTH NOTE (has a time value of one eighth of a whole note)

One eighth note looks like this.

When there are two eighth notes, their “flags” are joined.

SIXTEENTH NOTE (has a time value of one sixteenth of a whole note)

One sixteenth note looks like this.

When there are four sixteenth notes, their “flags” are joined.

Remember that a whole note = 2 half notes = 4 quarter notes = 8 eighth notes = 16 sixteenth notes.

The Rests: For each type of note there is a corresponding rest that has the same time value. A rest is a symbol that tells you when NOT to play. A rest should be counted in the beat of the music.

As with note values, a whole rest = 2 half rests = 4 quarter rests = 8 eighth rests = 16 sixteenth rests.

Repeat Signs: Watch your notation carefully for this symbol, which (in this book) indicates that you should go back to the beginning and repeat everything up to this symbol.

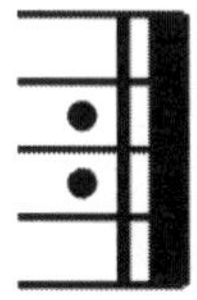

On a staff, a repeat sign looks like this:

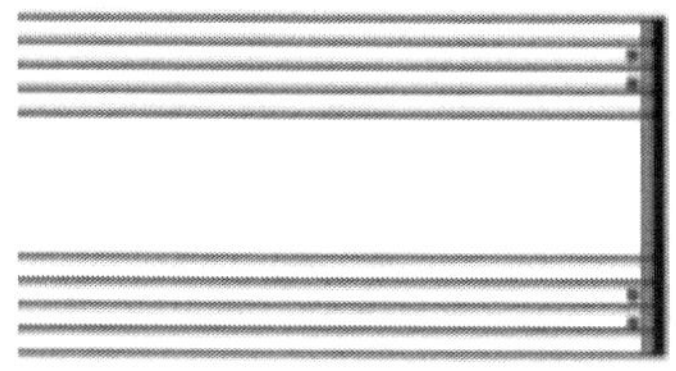

Brackets and Fingering: Brackets appear above certain groups of notes in the music notation. These indicate how you should place your fingers *in advance of actually plucking the strings.*

Your fingers are numbered thusly:
Thumb = 1
Index = 2
Middle = 3
Ring = 4

When you pre-place your fingers on the strings, and pluck in the order indicated, be careful not to lift off any fingers that have not plucked yet!

You cannot play accurately unless your fingers are pre-placed as indicated in the brackets. If you don't pre-place, you might pluck the wrong strings.

Fun Things to Do With Your Tiny Harp

If you tune to a pentatonic scale (see the options in the *How to Tune Your Tiny Harp* section), use a fingertip to strum from low to high strings, and your thumb to strum from high to low strings. This creates a lovely waterfall-like sound called a *glissando*, which is very pleasing. You can also pluck individual strings or groups of notes.

This playful way of using your harp is not the same as playing specific tunes such as the ones in this book, but it is a very pleasing way to use your harp until you learn how to play tunes.

Tunes for your Tiny Harp

The tunes are organized into three sections:

1. Tunes for One Hand for harps with 15 strings (from Middle C to High C)
2. Tunes for Two Hands for harps with 15 strings (from Middle C to High C)
3. Alternate Two-Hand Tunes for harps with 15 strings (from Middle C to High C)
4. Tunes for harps with 19 strings

Each section contains the simplest tunes first, and progresses to more complex ones.

Tunes for One Hand

15 Strings

For harps with strings from middle C to high C

Tha Mi Sgith (I Am So Tired)

Traditional Irish

Arr. by Laurie Riley and Lorna Govier

* This is a finger placing bracket: place your fingers on the strings before you play them. This technique is key to playing with ease and facility. In this case, place fingers 4 and 1 on the strings, then play the strings as shown in the music.

For harps with strings from middle C to high C

Give Me Your Hand

Rory Dall O'Cahan

Arr. by Laurie Riley and Lorna Govier

*Move lever up with left hand while right hand plays measure 45.

**Move lever down with left hand while right hand plays measure 46.

Tunes for Two Hands
15 Strings

For harps with strings from middle C to high C

Walking Fingers - Two Hands

Laurie Riley

Stems Up Right Hand, Stems Down Left Hand

Arr. by Lorna Govier

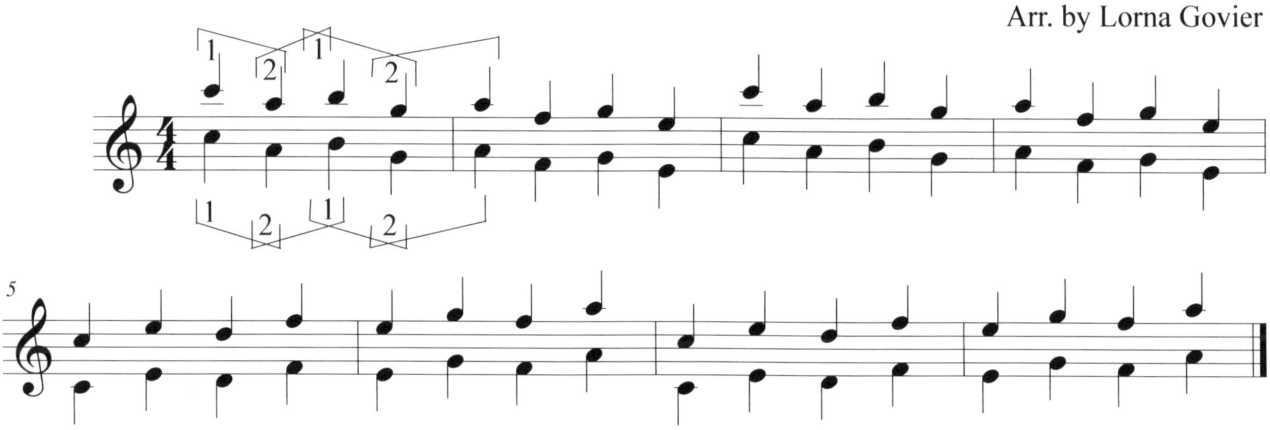

The Beginner's Waltz

Laurie Riley

Stems Up Right Hand, Stems Down Left Hand

Arr. by Lorna Govier

The Spider's Hornpipe

Laurie Riley

Stems Up Right Hand, Stems Down Left Hand

Arr. by Lorna Govier

Cathedral Bells

Laurie Riley

Stems Up Right Hand, Stems Down Left Hand

Arr. by Lorna Govier

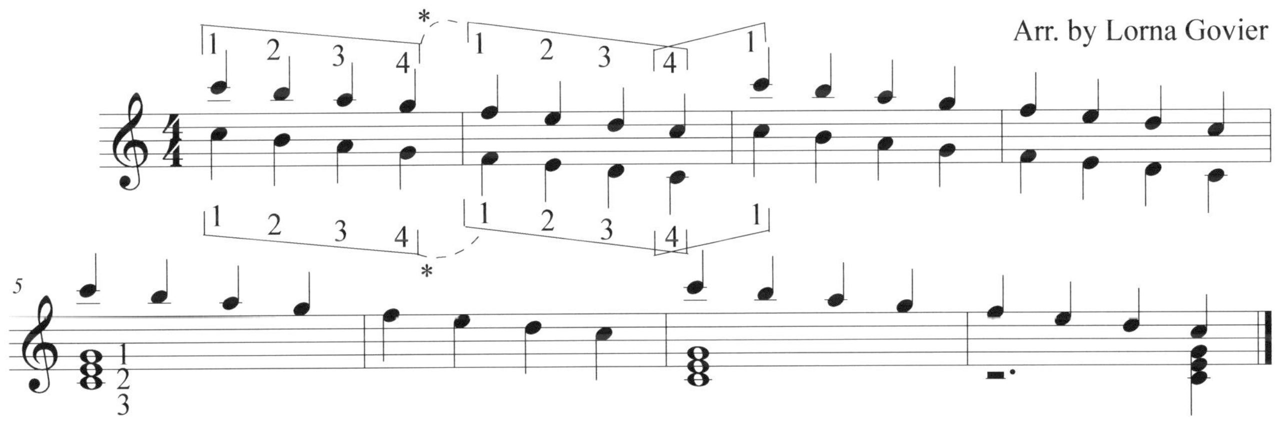

*Cross thumb over fourth finger, play finger 4 on G, then place fingers 2 on E, 3 on D, 4 on C.

Blossom Petals Falling

Laurie Riley

Stems Up Right Hand, Stems Down Left Hand

Arr. by Lorna Govier

For ease of reading standard notation on tiny harps, the treble clef will be used to represent notes played by both the right and left hand for the rest of this book.

Give Me Your Hand

Rory Dall O'Cahan

Arr. by Laurie Riley and Lorna Govier

17
21
25
29
33

* Move lever up with left hand while right hand plays measure 45.

** Move lever down with left hand while right hand plays measure 46.

For harps with strings from middle C to high C

Give Me Your Hand Version 2

Rory Dall O'Cahan

Arr. by Laurie Riley and Lorna Govier

17
21
25
29
33

Set F♮ lever; move lever down with left hand while right hand plays measure 45.

This page has been left blank to avoid an awkward page turn.

For harps with strings from middle C to high C

The Chanter's Tune

Traditional

Arr. by Laurie Riley and Lorna Govier

17
1 2 3 4
1 2 1
21
1 2 1

For harps with strings from middle C to high C

The Mist-Covered Mountains of Home

Traditional

Arr. by Laurie Riley and Lorna Govier

17
21
25
29

For harps with strings from middle C to high C

Lovely Joan

Traditional English

Arr. by Laurie Riley and Lorna Govier

For harps with strings from middle C to high C

Lovely Joan Version 2

Traditional

Arr. by Laurie Riley and Lorna Govier

For harps with strings from middle C to high C

Lovely Joan Version 3

Traditional

Arr. by Laurie Riley and Lorna Govier

This page has been left blank to avoid an awkward page turn.

For harps with strings from middle C to high C

Believe Me, If All Those Endearing Young Charms

Traditional
Words by Thomas Moore

Arr. by Lorna Govier

17
fair - y gifts fa - ding a - way,— Thou
21
wouldst still be ador'd as this mo - ment thou art, Let thy
25
love - li - ness fade as it will; And, a -
29
round the dear ru - in each wish of my heart Would en -
33
twine it - self ver - dant - ly still!

For harps with strings from middle C to high C

The Fairy Lullaby

Traditional

Arr. by Lorna Govier

This page has been left blank to avoid an awkward page turn.

For harps with strings from middle C to high C

Eleanor Plunkett

Turlough O'Carolan

Arr. by Laurie Riley and Lorna Govier

16
20
24
27
30

For harps with strings from middle C to high C

Eleanor Plunkett Version 2

Turlough O'Carolan

Arr. by Laurie Riley and Lorna Govier

16
20
24
27
30

For harps with strings from middle C to high C

Peat Fire Flame

Traditional

Arr. by Laurie Riley and Lorna Govier

17
21

For harps with strings from middle C to high C

Atholl Highlanders

Traditional

Stems Up Right Hand, Stems Down Left Hand

Arr. by Laurie Riley and Lorna Govier

For harps with strings from middle C to high C

Morrison's Jig

Traditional

Arr. by Laurie Riley and Lorna Govier

* This technique is called a "treble ornament". Place 4 on D, 1 on A. Your thumb will act as an anchor for your fingers as they rapidly play the D ornament: 4, 3 and 2. Do not close your fingers to your palm when playing the ornament - there isn't time! This is one of the few techniques where closing your fingers to your palm is not advisable.

Tunes for Two Hands

19 Strings

For harps with strings from G below middle C to D above high C

Eleanor Plunkett

Turlough O'Carolan

Arr. by Laurie Riley and Lorna Govier

16
20
24
27
30

Give Me Your Hand

Rory Dall O'Cahan

For Harps with Strings from G Below Middle C to B Below High C

Laurie Riley and Lorna Govier

17
21
25
29
33

37
41
Set F♮
45
49
53

For harps with strings from G below middle C to D above high C

Glenlivet

Traditional

Laurie Riley and Lorna Govier

For harps with strings from G below middle C to D above high C

Tha Mi Sgith (I Am So Tired)

Traditional Irish

Arr. by Laurie Riley and Lorna Govier

17
21
25
29

For harps with strings from middle C to D above high C

Lovely Joan

Traditional English

Laurie Riley and Lorna Govier

This page has been left blank to avoid an awkward page turn.

For harps with strings from G below middle C to D above high C

The Mist-Covered Mountains of Home

Traditional

Arr. by Laurie Riley and Lorna Govier

17
21
25
29

For harps with strings from G below middle C to D above high C

Morrison's Jig

Traditional

Laurie Riley and Lorna Govier

* This technique is called a "treble ornament". Place 4 on D, 1 on A. Your thumb will act as an anchor for your fingers as they rapidly play the D ornament: 4, 3 and 2. Do not close your fingers to your palm when playing the ornament - there isn't time! This is one of the few techniques where closing your fingers to your palm is not advisable.

This page has been left blank to avoid an awkward page turn.

For harps with strings from G below middle C to D above high C

Peat Fire Flame

Traditional

Arr. by Laurie Riley and Lorna Govier

17
21

For harps with strings from G below middle C to D above high C

The Chanter's Tune

Traditional

Laurie Riley and Lorna Govier

17
21

For harps with strings from G below middle C to B below high C

Give Me Your Hand

Rory Dall O'Cahan

Laurie Riley and Lorna Govier

17
21
25
29
33

37
41
Set F♮ lever; move lever down with left hand while right hand plays measure 45.
45
49
53